Heartfelt

"After the death of my babies, I reached a point where I no longer wanted to live. Heartfelt came to my rescue. I will never forget it."

— Debbie McMahon, La Puente, California

♥

"After the death of my son, I felt that I was losing my mind. What Heartfelt taught me about the stages of grief helped me to survive."

— Linda R. Garza, Pomona, California

♥

"The death of my baby made me feel hopeless, angry, and confused. Heartfelt helped me begin the process of understanding and healing my grief. I am able to keep the memory of my child alive, and for this I am eternally grateful."

— Leslie Cline, Sierra Madre, California

♥

Heartfelt

A COMPANION FOR BEREAVED PARENTS

Jeri Rae Miller

Cypress House

Heartfelt:
A Companion for Bereaved Parents

Cypress House
155 Cypress Street
Fort Bragg, CA 95437
(800) 773-7782
www.cypresshouse.com

Cover and book design: Michael Brechner/Cypress House

Library of Congress Cataloging-in-Publication Data

Miller, Jeri Rae, 1936-
Heartfelt : a companion for bereaved parents / Jeri Rae Miller.
p. cm.
ISBN-13: 978-1-879384-74-3 (pbk. : alk. paper)
1. Children--Death--Psychological aspects. 2. Grief. 3. Loss (Psychology) 4. Bereavement--Psychological aspects. I. Title.
BF575.G7M534 2006
155.9'37--dc22

2006020215

Printed in the USA
2 4 6 8 9 7 5 3 1

In memory of my son,
Christian Jay Miller,
without whose life and death
I would not be the woman I am today.

♥

Preface

In this book, I will share with you what I've learned about parental grief from personal experience in surviving the death of my young son and in the twenty-one years I spent counseling thousands of bereaved parents who have endured the loss of a child.

I begin with my own story from a mother's perspective, and then provide chapters from my family, portraying a father's grief and the feelings of my son's sisters and brother.

I give you a road map through the grief process, starting with a discussion of the stages of grief and then offer suggestions for living through these stages and completing the process. I hope this will help lessen your pain during such a terrible time.

Of course, your life may never be the same, and the pain may never go away completely, but my central message is that you can make the right choices, and learn the best way to deal with your grief, and if you do,

You Will Survive and You Will Smile Again

♥

With heartfelt love and compassion,
Jeri Rae Miller

Contents

♥

Chapter 1

♥

Introduction

At last . . . it was the day my husband and I were leaving on a much-needed mini-vacation: five days in Las Vegas. The date was March 2, 1976.

Here we were, Jess, my husband, a busy, hard-working, successful attorney, and also senior partner in his law firm, and me, a busy homemaker with five children and a stepson to care for. But my big fortieth had just occurred on February 16. That's enough to make anyone ready for "Time Out!"

Our children were Nancy, twenty-three, who was married to Craig, with my first grandchild, Jared, and another baby due in June, who were living in Visalia at the time.

Cynthia, eighteen, was living at home and was helping Rosie, the nanny we had hired to help tend the younger children while we made our escape. My mother was also available to help if she was needed.

Craig, twenty, my stepson, was living in northern California.

Steven, seventeen, was living at home and attending high school.

Traci, thirteen, was in middle school and just entering the wonderful world of teenagers.

Christian, seven, was in second grade.

Steven and Christian took us to LAX to fly off for five days of fun, relaxation, lying in the sun and, naturally, some gambling.

Never did I consider, as Jess and I got out of our Buick station wagon, and Steve and Christian waved goodbye as we entered the airport, that that would be the last time I would see my beautiful blond-brown, curly-haired, lanky, green-eyed Christian alive.

In Las Vegas we were staying at the MGM Grand, which was then one of the newer hotel-casinos in Las Vegas.

Americans everywhere in the United States seemed to be in a festive mood: it was 1976, and we were celebrating the bicentennial.

It was the last thing, for a long time, that I would celebrate; the last time I would feel the freedom to celebrate anything.

When we arrived in our room, I immediately called home, as was my usual practice, to check in and see how everyone was doing and tell them that we had arrived safely.

That was on a Tuesday. Jess and I swam and lazed around the pool during the day, and gambled late into the night on Tuesday and Wednesday.

We went to see Teresa Brewer perform that night, Wednesday, at the Stardust Hotel. I had always enjoyed her singing, and we had great fun.

The beginning of hell arrived the next day.

♥

Chapter 2

Hell on Earth

Thursday, March 4, started off as another fun-filled day and ended with a horrible nightmare that is still indescribable nearly thirty years later.

We arose that Thursday morning, went down to the dining area to have breakfast, and, after we had eaten, we gambled for a few hours. It was 1:30 or so, and Jess said that he needed to phone his office and some clients, so I went with him to our room. I wasn't having any luck at gambling anyway.

Jess started making his calls. I was sitting on the sofa, reading a novel I'd started a couple of days earlier, when Jerry, law partner and friend, broke in with an emergency call.

I looked at Jess and saw him turn as white as a sheet. Jess looked at me and said, "Chris has been hit by a car. His nose is bleeding and he's unconscious!"

What did Jess say? This can't be happening! Chris is at his friend David's house, waiting for his brother to pick him up and bring him home.

Oh my God, we have to get home! I was running around the hotel room, crying, shaking, unable to think straight.

Jess came over, put his arms around my quaking body, and gently said, "Honey, I don't think our baby Christian is going to make it!"

"Yes," I cried, "he will be fine—don't tell me that!"

Let's just get home—have to get home—so far away—opening and closing the dresser drawers—throwing things into my suitcase—Home—so far away—I can't think—my head is spinning—my hands are trembling—going to be sick. No, I can't be sick, I have to hurry and get home.

"Chris will be just fine," I keep telling myself as I'm throwing my things into my suitcase, certainly not my usual everything-in-its-place, neat way of packing.

Down in the lobby now checking out, whimpering, not believing what was happening. Hurry, my mind said, we *have* to hurry, *have* to get home, *driven* to get home. *Where's* a cab?

At last we found a cab and were driven to the Las Vegas Airport. I got out, ran to the ticket counter, and told the women there, "We must have two tickets now! Our son has been struck by a car." My thoughts were going wild. Have to get home!

They, whoever they were, had taken Chris to San Gabriel Hospital near the San Gabriel Mission. "He'll be okay," the lady behind the ticket counter says, smiling kindly, trying to calm me.

"Who is this happening to?" my mind screamed in disbelief. "Not me, not Jess, not my Chris. Hurry, we have to get on the plane."

Once we board, I sit next to an older man. Jess is on the other side of me. The plane is on the ground for an eternity. What's happening? *What did Jerry say?* my tormented mind keeps repeating. No, don't think that, he's fine, just a broken arm.

I start crying again. The man next to me asks why I'm crying. I tell him, sobbing, "My son has been hit by a car and we need to get home." He replies, "Oh, don't cry, I've had three children die. Just snap out of it!"

I jumped up and ran up and down the aisle. I had to get away from that horrible man. How dare he suggest that my baby could possibly be that hurt, let alone dead! Nowhere to run.

Jess is following me. The flight attendant finds us seats in the back of the plane. We sit. Jess takes my trembling hand. His is also trembling. We're in shock.

Look at Jess. He looks so afraid and so very sad. "Don't be scared," I say, "Chris is fine." Jess looks at me with tears in his eyes. *Please God, let him be okay.*

Please, my mind cries out again and again. The flight attendant comes and asks if she can do anything to help. I plead with her to have the pilot call ahead for a police car to take us to the hospital—to our baby boy. She leaves, then comes back and assures us that a car will be waiting for us at LAX. Okay, I think. Now things are getting under control. *Please, please, let him be okay, God, I'll do anything, just please let him be okay.*

He's so little, so pure and sweet. *Oh, shut up, Jeri,* I tell myself. Of course, he's just fine. Where are my other children? Wait! I called them before we left the hotel. Cynthia answered the phone. I said, "Cindy, what's happened?" She was crying. She didn't know. Traci and Cindy were the only ones home. She told me one of our neighbors was going to take her and Traci to the hospital. "Okay," I said. "I love you. Dad and I are on our way home." *Where's Steve? Oh my God, this can't be happening, not to us, my kids are my life.*

Poor Jess looks shattered. The plane is landing now—hurry. I have to go and find the police car while Jess collects our luggage. I'm outside, looking all around—no police car in sight. I run back into the airport and tell Jess to hurry. It's 6 p.m., over three hours since we got that awful phone call from Jerry. What did Jerry say again?

No! He's wrong! Chris's nose couldn't be bleeding. *Stop!* Don't think about that! We have to get a cab. We're finally in the back seat of the cab. "Hurry," Jess tells the driver, "our son has been hit by a car and we have to get to San Gabriel Hospital."

"Where's that?" the driver asks. Jess looks at me and asks, "Where's the hospital?" Oh, my God. I can't think—my mind is whirling. It's getting dark. Have to hurry. Can't think. *Must* think. Where is the hospital? Finally, I tell him how to get there. Please, please, hurry. An hour later, we pull up to the emergency entrance of the hospital. I jump out of the car and run in while Jess is paying the cab driver.

In the hospital everything is so clean and white. There's a nurse coming toward me. "I'm Mrs. Miller," I cry. "Where is my son Chris?" She looks at me with a look all parents dread, and I cry out. My legs won't hold me up—my body is failing me. My world and life as I had known them were forever altered at that moment.

After Jess entered the hospital, the nurse took us into a small room and I said, "Where is our son?" She looked at us and said, "He's in the morgue!" Just like that. I didn't know what to say. That nurse crushed my heart, my soul. The essence of my being went numb and my body quaked as if I were on a vibrating machine. I wailed, sounds of primal anguish. Then she looked at me and said, "Well, you have other children, don't you?" As if one child could possibly make up for the death of another. Then she offered to get us some pills to help control our emotions, when the only thing that would ever make it all right was for Christian to walk into the room. But no—he was gone! Some huge bird with huge talons had plucked him off the planet! We sat in the hospital hallway and waited for Jerry to come take us home to our other children.

We drove up to the front of our home. I got out with Jess and Jerry, and when the door opened, all our kids were standing there. I said, "Where's Chris?" And then it hit me all over again, and I collapsed. I was to find out in the hours, days, and months to follow that this was just the beginning of the grief process.

The disbelief and then the truth of what had occurred would sweep over me, the horrible feelings of incredulity, incredible sadness, unstoppable wailing, and moaning for the loss of my sweet baby son Christian.

♥

Chapter 3

♥

My Thoughts

The days following Chris's accident were like plodding through thick, dark mud. My thoughts were slow, yet at the same time swift. My head was spinning, my world was upside down. Everything I deemed "normal" wasn't anymore. My life had been upended. The normal sequence of life was out of order, out of sync. Parents aren't supposed to outlive their children. The days that followed were literally that—*a daze*. I remember going to church after church with Jess and some of my kids, trying, searching for comfort and some kind of answer to make any sense out of this topsy-turvy world I was now stuck in. Ultimately, I went back to my childhood religion for peace and comfort, and Jess did whatever he had to do to find his level of solace, but none of that would come for a very long while. In this interaction among my husband and me and our other children, I learned that the grief process is one of the most intimate, private things one goes through.

Grief is one of the most personal things anyone can endure. And they must go through it in their own time and in their own way. You cannot tell anyone else how to grieve. It's a long, hard, tumultuous time in anyone's life.

The death of a child is devastating.

After a year of searching for a support group, or for anyone who had lost a child, I decided to do something with the incredible pain that I was in. I took my idea, which was to form a support group for parents whose children had died, regardless of age or the circumstances surrounding the death, to Huntington Memorial Hospital in Pasadena, California. The Patient Service Staff were thrilled at the possibility of having a support group available for grieving parents and so Heartfelt was born.

♥

Chapter 4

The Birth of Heartfelt

I didn't know the first thing about starting an organization. All I knew was that I felt a tremendous need for one. I needed to be around people who were experiencing similar feelings associated with the death of their child or children.

Heartfelt was born in November 1977, almost two years after the death of my Christian. In the beginning, I held monthly meetings in the hospital's conference rooms, but I soon became aware of the parents' discomfort and my own. The familiarity of the hospital and its smells were all too fresh, reminding parents of their painful experience in this environment, so I decided to move the meetings to my home in San Marino, California. I was being trained by the counselors at Huntington Memorial Hospital and soon became a certified grief counselor.

In the beginning, just a few parents showed up, but after a while, we were overflowing with parents. It was sometimes overwhelming to be in the presence of so much pain, but I put aside my own pain to help the newly bereaved parents, and in doing so, discovered that I was being supported in return. This was another of the valuable lessons I was to start learning along my path to being healed and also to become the president and founder of Heartfelt Support Group, Inc.

I held meetings on the third Monday evening of every month and offered telephone support 24/7, 365 days a year. I never wanted any parent to be unable to reach out and get help when they decided that was their need. Some bereaved parents will search for support immediately, as was the case with my husband and me, or they may wait a few months or a year. Everyone is different. I had no idea that there was such a thing as the grief process, but I would soon discover that the feelings I had experienced from the moment I learned of my son's death were entirely normal—normal, that is, for the grief process to begin its unwelcome journey through my life and my family's lives as well.

The stages of grief are usually right on the mark, one usually following another in sequence, but not necessarily. I thought in the beginning that there would be a difference if a family had lost a child through miscarriage, as opposed to losing one after the child had been here for a while, but that notion was soon dispelled. In fact, in the beginning, more parents who had experienced a miscarriage or a stillbirth were coming to Heartfelt than were parents of older children.

When, in the year 1998, I retired from Heartfelt, I had operated and facilitated it on my own for twenty-one years, and had created five other Heartfelt chapters around the country, and a much-needed Spanish-speaking chapter as well. Our monthly newsletter reached more than 4,000 parents.

Heartfelt also provided training for parents who, a year removed from their loss, chose to stay and become "Support

Parents" to help newly bereaved parents through the incredible loss they had recently suffered. We also offered one-on-one telephone-support counseling and a 24-hour hotline, and had created an annual Heartfelt picnic. After more than twenty years of providing service to bereaved parents, I knew that from the death of my son, Christian, a great many bereaved parents had found solace and support by participating in Heartfelt during the time of their grief. Heartfelt was a wonderful tribute to my Chris's memory. What a difference his life had made.

Grief fills the room up of my absent child,
Lies in his bed, walks up and down with me,
Puts on his pretty looks, repeats his words,
Remembers me of all his gracious parts,
Stuffs out his vacant garments with his form.
Then have I reason to be fond of grief?
Fare you well: had you such a loss as I,
I could give better comfort than you do.

— William Shakespeare, *King John*

♥

Chapter 5

Father's Grief

Jess Miller

Most of what I know about a father's grief I learned the hard way, from the loss of my beloved son, Christian, and my struggle through the grief process. The rest I learned through the work of my wonderful wife, who dealt with thousands of families who had experienced the loss of a child, and the reading that I've done on this subject in preparation for the Father's Day talks that I later gave at Heartfelt meetings.

I, like you, remember the horror of that moment when we learned our son had been taken from us. The unmistakable look on the face of the doctor when we arrived at the hospital following Christian's accident; my pounding on the doctor's chest and screaming, "Tell me there is a God"; the terrified and hopeless look on my wife's face; the dazed sense of being awake but feeling as if I were in a horrible dream; the days, weeks, and months that followed with both Jeri and me in a state of helplessness, shock, and despair; the pulling myself together to remain composed so I could try to comfort everyone, including my children and friends. At times, I would go out in our yard and shout curses to the fates that would do such a thing to such a wonderful little boy, feeling that I wanted to find the driver of the car, who was not at fault, and inflict serious bodily harm in retaliation for what he had taken from me. Irrational thoughts flooded my mind, like believing Chris would appear at any time, thinking that if I could only lie down and die that he would be all right, or at least I would be next to him; dreaming that if only I could have fifteen more minutes with him alive, everything would be okay and I could be taken as well.

I remember the efforts of friends to console me. Sometimes their well-meaning words only angered me, such as their saying, "Everything will be all right in time," or "At least you have your other children." Some even compared what I was experiencing to their loss of a pet, and I just wanted to punch them. I recall being consoled to an extent by a few friends who said, "Chris was a wonderful boy, we loved him and we love you." As time passed, however, I noticed I was more able to talk to others about Chris. I remember most the kind words of people I didn't know whose lives he had touched: the service-station owner at a garage near Chris's school, who wrote a letter to us and said what a wonderful little boy he was; and the cafeteria worker at Chris's school, who sent us a note saying how much she had come to love Chris, because he would always come in and volunteer to help her set up the cafeteria before lunch. There were others whom I've forgotten over time.

I need to tell you a little bit about how much Chris meant to me, to Jeri, and to our family. Chris, whom I called Christian when he was naughty (yes, there were times when he wasn't perfect), was the linchpin of our family. Both Jeri and I had been married previously and had children from those marriages. Christian was our only child together, and was thus the only child related by blood to all the other children in the family. Christian's brothers and sisters adored him. I have to mention here that the word "stepchild" or "step" anything is not in my vocabulary. I've loved all of our children as deeply as any parent could love a child, and have been blessed by the return of that love.

Christian was a very active little guy. We played baseball together. His favorite expression when he'd hit a particularly long ball was, "I slammed that one, Daddy, didn't I?" We rode our bikes all over San Marino, the Huntington Library grounds, the parks, and I treasure those memories. We would stop at the high school sometimes and watch people play tennis. Christian said he wanted to play when he got older, and we were planning on lessons for him. He could swim before he could walk. He loved costumes and wasn't embarrassed to be out in public costumed as Batman, a cowboy, a policeman, or a soldier. He was left-handed, and that was wonderful to me since no one else in our family was, and I just knew that he was going to grow up to be the next Sandy Koufax. He knew how to order food. When we'd go to a restaurant, he had a routine: he'd simply repeat, "Shrimp cocktail, extra sauce, prime rib, medium-rare, extra au jus." Maybe he was a little spoiled, but I wish we'd spoiled him more. He loved fishing and would proudly announce whatever anyone else had caught: "That's a striper, that's a perch," whatever the fish may have been. He wasn't always right, but we thought it was cute. He would tell us naughty little jokes that a seven-year-old would pick up at school, and he always looked so devilish when he told them. One, for example, was that he said he could always play baseball because he had a bat, two balls, and a catcher's mitt, pointing at his bottom.

Over the months and years following our loss of Chris (I still have difficulty saying "death"), I learned a lot about the grieving process. Initially, I can remember being resentful of all the attention showered on Jeri, the mother, while I, the father, was expected to be brave and not need the sympathy of others. This was a selfish feeling, and, fortunately, I soon got over it. I believe that the mother should be treated more gently, but I continue to believe that it should be recognized that fathers grieve just as much, and need some of the loving attention often denied them at this critical time. But that different treatment of the father and the mother is really an indicator of the fact that fathers grieve differently than mothers do. Of course, their pain is just as deep, but society has placed different expectations on how each should behave following the death of a child. In addition, something in the makeup of men and women differentiates how they'll react to a horrible loss. It's important to recognize this difference, and particularly important for both mother and father to understand that the other will not grieve in precisely the manner that he or she will, and to allow each to grieve in his or her own special way.

Both mother and father go through the various roadblocks along the way to some kind of recovery. Each will experience, in no particular order, the various phases: believing they're going crazy, not knowing they're in total shock, denying and disbelieving that the loss is true, being unable to sleep, having wide mood swings, losing appetite, questioning long-held beliefs, and feeling isolated—even stigmatized among friends and coworkers, who are embarrassed and don't know what to say. Religion can help, but in our case it wasn't nearly enough.

I haven't yet mentioned the guilt that parents feel. We beat ourselves up because we went on vacation. What were we doing vacationing, even though we had adequately provided for Christian's care? Even if we'd been there, it's unlikely that anything would have changed, since Chris was in his regular car pool. We have to forgive ourselves, because there's not one of us who wouldn't change things if we could. In reality, we are seldom really responsible to the point that we should feel guilty about whatever happened to our child. Forgiving oneself is vital.

Fathers usually must grieve inside themselves, alone, except for the crucial interchange with their wives. Friends and relatives are less prone to focus attention, sympathy, and support on the father. The prevailing (inaccurate) view is that he needs it less than Mom does.

Contributing to the difference in dealing with grief of the mother and father is the macho image that some men feel they must have. The notion that men can't cry—certainly not in public—is a fallacy. Men have to cry sometimes, and there's nothing wrong with it, public or private. You must allow yourself to cry. Men feel they need to be the protector of their wife at this time, and may often say insensitive things. For example, if a man can't stop his wife from crying, or if her grieving continues longer than he thinks is good for her, it's easy to say something like "Honey, it's been six months" (or whatever period is involved). "Don't you think it's time you stopped crying?" What he really means is "Honey, I don't know how to comfort you; I'm doing the best I can, and that's why I say what I say."

A neighbor came up to me at the funeral, hugged me at a time when I was about to break down, and told me, "Jess, you've got to be strong." I realized that I did have to be strong, and hold in check the unbearable grief I was feeling, so I pulled myself together and grieved later, privately. Had I broken down just then, there could have been a domino effect on my wife and children.

Often, a father feels more guilt than the mother, because of the mistaken notion that he is the guardian of the family and has failed in not keeping his child alive. This is not healthy, nor is it based in rational thinking, even though we men probably all go through it.

A matter that often arose in Heartfelt meetings, as parents shared their feelings with others who had experienced a similar loss, was the fact that men sometimes wanted to turn to sex with their wives much sooner than their wives were ready. The wives felt, "How could he do that or want that at a time like this?" In reality, he was trying to express his love for her in the only way that he could at the time.

During the course of our involvement with Heartfelt, the literature and the experience of others revealed to us that many parents divorce following the loss of a child. One might think that such a loss should, if anything, bring the parents closer together, but it often results in precisely the opposite. In my opinion, the main reason for this is that the parents do not give each other room to grieve in their own individual ways, and frustration and resentment develop between them.

We were very fortunate, because each of us seemed to understand intuitively the need to let the other react to our loss in his or her own way. For example, Jeri felt a need to know exactly how Chris's accident had happened, and she got the police reports and talked to neighbors to find out. To this day, almost thirty years later, I don't know the precise details of Chris's death, and didn't want to know for years afterward. Jeri and I both had a hard time referring to it, and we both used some euphemism such as his "accident." She was able to adjust to that a lot sooner than I was. For years I never said he "died," only that he had been taken from us or that we had lost him.

At his memorial service, Jeri could not view his body. I, on the other hand, was compelled to view him, kiss him, and be with him in those last few moments when I could envision him on earth. We understood each other, and we supported each other better as a result. Jeri goes to the cemetery much more often than I do. To this day, she feels Chris's warmth or presence more than I do, and it helps her. I think she understands that my not going is not an indication that I love or miss Chris any less.

Among the lessons I learned along the way is that the way in which the child died does not diminish the severity of the pain felt by the parents. Initially, I thought that only someone who had lost a beautiful seven-and-a-half-year-old boy could possibly know what I was going through or deserved the same attention that I needed. Whether the death is through stillbirth, death in adulthood, suicide, miscarriage, accident, or illness, no parent ever expects to experience so unnatural an event as having a child die. The pain and loss goes to your very soul, regardless of how the child was lost. Another lesson lay in my failure to recognize the pain of others besides the mother and father. Brothers and sisters, grandparents, aunts and uncles, and others will also be in pain as a result of the loss of a loved one. Their needs, often overlooked, should be given more attention than they usually are.

As time passes, a day comes when you begin to recover and resume a normal life. Nothing ever felt entirely normal about life after the loss of my child, but it surprised me how close

I could come to it. You may, as I did, begin to feel a perverse kind of guilt, because you're not grieving as much anymore, and not thinking about your child as much as you feel you should. Again, it's important to allow yourself forgiveness for letting your own life go on while your child's does not.

In the throes of your deepest grief, it's hard to believe that there will come a time when you start feeling better, but if you make the right choices, and get the support you need, I promise that you'll survive and enjoy living again. It might never feel totally complete, but you'll smile and have good times again. You'll relate to your child with mixed feelings of pleasure and pain, and the pleasure eventually overcomes the pain. You'll begin to think pleasant thoughts and enjoy your beautiful memories of your child. You can imagine with some pleasure that your child might have been a movie star, a doctor, president of the United States, or a big-league ball player. You can look at old photos with great joy or listen to old recordings of your child's voice. We've got photos and some film from the days we had our Chris. We have only one recording of his voice, which we made one Saturday morning when he jumped into our bed when he was only six years old. I told him to get my dictation unit from my office, and we recorded a silly little thing: I announced a show, in which he sang and recited several poems including "Ladles and Jellyspoons." I treasure and safeguard that tape. I can't listen to it without crying tears of joy.

You can look upon your experience and benefit from it. You have a clearer perspective on the important things, which can lead you to improve your own life. I am certain that Jeri and I are better people than we would have been otherwise, and we have done more to help others than we would have. Jeri has helped thousands through Heartfelt.

The death of a child has influenced a number of famous people to comment on how important that loss was in their lives. Authors Joseph Wambaugh and Dominick Dunne have injected traces of it into almost all of their writing. Helen Hayes, one of the greatest actresses in the history of theater and film, and winner of numerous international awards and Oscars, was asked in her late eighties what was the most significant thing about her. Her answer was, in effect, "I survived the loss of my child."

If someone were to ask me what was the most significant thing about me, I would certainly have to consider answering, "I had a son named Chris."

♥

Chapter 6

♥

Letters from Siblings

Three of my children, who were living in our family home at the time of my Chris's death, have written their thoughts for this book. I'm deeply grateful for their efforts to put on paper the emotions that they went through.

From Cynthia

I remember it as if it were yesterday. My parents had gone on a trip to Las Vegas and we had a baby-sitter staying with us. I was eighteen and a senior in high school. My brother, Steven, was seventeen and a junior in high school, and my younger sister, Traci, was thirteen and a seventh grader in middle school. Last but certainly not least, there was Chris, our beloved younger brother who was seven and in second grade.

That dreadful day when my baby brother was struck down and killed by a gardener's truck is one that I will never, ever forget. Being the older sister, I remember Chris asking me to make him some pancakes. I remember being a little angry about it because I was in a hurry to get to school and to a doctor's appointment, I made the spoiled brat his precious pancakes. He had to have been one of the pickiest eaters ever. I am so glad, though, that I made him his breakfast that last morning of his life, because I felt just as bad for getting angry with him. It took me a long time to forgive myself the anger.

Later in the day, I went to my eye doctor and had my eyes dilated. As I sat there in the chair before my examination, something inside me, a small still voice, was nagging at me, telling me that I had to get home, just had to get home, that something was wrong. With that intuition, I got up from the chair, eyes dilated, dark glasses on, and drove home. Just as I was turning the corner to my house, I saw an ambulance driving away, sirens and all, and I just knew that something was terribly wrong. I did not know exactly what, but I knew it was something horrible.

When I entered our home, my brother, Steve, was there with a neighbor offering to drive us to the hospital because Chris had been hit by a car. I remember shrieking the most horrific scream, and my disbelief of what had happened to him was paralyzing. I was asking where Traci was, and asking a million questions about what had happened, and the phone was ringing off the hook.

I remember staying home to wait for Traci and to await the arrival of my mom and dad.

Steve went to the hospital and waited for my parents to arrive. What happened next is an unbelievable, painful memory that I can hardly sit here and type without crying and drying my tears every minute. To see your mom and dad cry and scream and shout for days on end has to be the worst feeling ever. I felt so powerless, unable to help them.

To see my precious, loving mom sitting in her chair, crying

and crying, and smoking one cigarette after another, with no food for days, is so painful that I could only hope and pray that I would never have to live through that kind of grief. I remember my mom not eating; she would say, "My precious Chris isn't eating, and I can't either." I saw her shrink to half her size. I had my own pain and suffering to go through as a sister, but to see my parents so racked with pain was almost too much to bear.

As time went on, it only became more and more apparent that this horrific pain and suffering would last a long, long time. My poor mother became so afraid to let each of her remaining children out of her sight for fear of something happening to the rest of us.

As time passed, my mom came to me one day and said, "I have other children to live for, and I must go on and live my life for you!" I remember feeling great relief in that statement. Not that I wanted to ever forget Chris, but I wanted my mom back, and I wanted her love and security. It was very scary to not have my mom's full love and attention.

As for my dad, I remember him handling the grief and pain very differently. One day he just started back to work and lived life in his routine. I'm sure it was his way of coping and just not breaking apart. He is amazing. How he ever coped with this loss is something I will never understand.

The passing of my beloved brother, Chris, is something that will always leave a mark in my life. It taught me early on that we can come and go so quickly and we have no say in the matter. Life is precious, and we have to live it to the fullest.

I am so proud of my parents that they were able to stay together after such a tragedy. My mother started a support group for bereaved parents that lasted for over twenty years. My father supported her every step of the way and contributed to many special "Father's Day" meetings to help other fathers cope with their grief. I'm so proud of the two of them. They have lived through a tragedy that no one wants to ever have to face. They have lived it and survived.

I dedicate my story to my loving brother, Chris, and to my loving parents, Jeri and Jesse, whom I will adore for eternity.

With all my love,

Cynthia

From Steven

I never could have imagined how perfect and beautiful a baby brother could be. Chris was a living plaything. I had such plans for him and me. I wanted to teach him to do things that I'd had to discover on my own, shortcut the time it would take him to learn them.

Together, Chris and I were going to conquer the world in outdoor activities and physical challenges. He was my "Bud" man. He inspired me to do things in a way that I never would have if it weren't for his inspiration. I was just beginning to teach him about backpacking. We went camping in Eaton Canyon. He drew me a picture of that experience. I knew it meant a lot to him, not only because of the picture, but by the good time he had camping with me.

I remember one time riding bicycles with Chris. I was so confident in his ability to overcome physical challenges that I told him he was fully capable of riding his bike down this steep hill and stopping before he slammed into a wall. He believed it too. Unfortunately, he was just a little boy and not fully ready to handle sliding a bike sideways while applying the brakes and avoiding the wall at the same time. He hit the wall hard and almost flew over it into the wash!

I was so upset with myself for talking him into doing that. But the fact that he did it demonstrated to me how much he trusted me and my judgment.

I don't feel I ever took Chris for granted. I loved every moment we had together. Whether we were riding bikes (I taught him to ride), hiking, swimming, playing baseball, or just hanging out together; those times we had were some of the most precious gifts of my life.

At the end of our lives, all we're going to have are the memories. My memories of Chris are infinite. They're like a tape of your favorite movie that you can play over and over again. And every time you play it, you see or hear something new.

How often do we really think about the things we do with that much detail? Not often.

Losing Chris at such a young age was both a tragedy and a blessing, all at the same time.

When I die, I'll know that I knew my brother Chris very well.

Steven

From Traci

I'm wondering, will Mom be angry with me because I'm in detention again? It's only for chewing gum…this school is so strict. Why is my neighbor here? They come over to where I'm sitting and very lovingly tell me I need to leave—there's been an accident in my family. I walked outside and she told me that Chris had been hit by a car and I needed to go home. It didn't really sink in. Chris? My brother? Or Chris, my neighbor? I couldn't think that it would be my brother. We drove down Lombardy Road, and I saw the man, saw his grief-stricken face. I saw the truck, I saw the place where Chris was just taken from. I saw the neighbor who let Chris out in the middle of the street, saw her put her hands to her face and start screaming. I was wondering, *What is going on?*

I'm taken home and I sit on the front porch steps waiting for someone to come home. Here comes Cindy, my sister, she has funny glasses over her eyes. She asked why I was on the steps. I told her that Chris had been hit by a car, and she started to cry. Our other neighbor came over and got Cindy and me, and we drove to the hospital where Chris had been taken. Cindy got out of the car and told me to stay and wait. I was in the front seat when I saw my brother, Steve, coming out. I saw him and Cindy hugging each other and crying. *What is happening? Why won't anyone tell me?* They get to the car and tell me that Chris has died. A car hit him. I'm in shock. After that, I really don't recall much. I remember going home and running away to a friend's house and telling her that my brother died. I wanted to stay there. Someone found me and took me home just in time to see my mom and dad coming back from their weekend trip.

I remember my mom collapsing as she came in the door. The rest is unclear. The pain and suffering and crying in the house were too hard for me to bear. I took myself away and stayed at my aunt's home. I had never stayed with her or even had a relationship with her, but I just wanted not to be home. I remember going with my grandma to view Chris, and I remember she kissed Chris on the cheek and said, "That's from your mother." I started to cry a lot then. I put my necklace in the casket with Chris. He had his Pooh Bear with him. He never went anywhere without his Pooh Bear. My dad was there. I remember him in the hearse with Chris. I thought *He is being so protective of Chris.*

I had a hard time because I felt a lot of guilt. I remember the day of the funeral when my aunt tried to get me dressed. I ran away when I saw my mom going to the casket and kissing it goodbye. My brother, Steven, had to come after me, and then I got a horrible nosebleed. Back at the house after the funeral, my uncle told me I didn't need to eat that much. I was totally upset with him for saying that. What does it matter what I eat? Chris is gone. Forever. After that day, our family went to the cemetery where we buried Chris, and the rest has become pretty much a blur to me.

I dealt with my pain by running away. I didn't want to deal with it. I had always had a weight problem growing up, and then one day I woke up and all my weight was gone. I don't even know how it happened. I remember going back to school, and one boy teased me so badly and said that Chris died because of me, that it was all my fault. I was hysterical at that point, and told my teacher, and my dad came and picked me up, and the next day the principal of the school let him speak to that boy. I don't know exactly what my dad said, but from that day on, no one ever bothered me again. They didn't tease me about my weight or say anything about Chris.

In therapy years later, I discovered that I felt so much guilt, because the night before Chris died we got into a fight, as siblings often do, over the TV remote control. I threw it at him and it hit his forehead, and I said, "I hate you so much I just wish you would die." Well, the next day, Chris passed away. It took me ten years to discover why I felt so much pain and grief. I understood why I was so hysterical about what that boy at school had said. There's an empty feeling in the house when someone is gone. I used to be very uncomfortable when my mom or my dad would cry. I would go with my mom to visit Chris, and I used to hate it when I'd see her cry while she was putting the flowers on Chris's grave and the pinwheel in the ground. I always felt so bad because I didn't know what to say or do. Then Mom would be so quiet on the drive home.

One thing I've learned because of Chris's death is never to end any conversation without saying, "I love you." No matter how angry I am, I try very hard to overcome that anger, and instead say, "I love you." You just never know what can happen. Life has a way of throwing zingers at you, and it takes you so much by surprise that it literally takes your breath away. But you learn to deal with it, just like we had to learn to deal with Chris's death. You never forget. But you soon start to heal from the pain. Each day it gets a little easier.

Then one day, ten years had passed, and I found myself lying on the grass next to Chris asking for his forgiveness for being such a brat the night before he died. Then in the coolness of that March day, with white puffy clouds in the sky, I fell asleep in the peace of knowing, at that moment, that my heart was healed and Chris was there to love me.

Traci

♥

Chapter 7

♥

The Grieving Process: Stages of Grief

The order in which we experience reactions to the death of a child varies from person to person. But we can all expect to deal with almost all of the following stages of grief as we make our way through the grieving process. They will occur in no particular order and sometimes will overlap.

Stages of Grief

- Shock
- Disbelief
- Anger
- Feelings of guilt
- Feelings that you're going crazy
- Feelings of despair

- ♥ Feelings of overwhelming sadness
- ♥ No feelings, emotional numbness

As we go through these stages, we will encounter some or all of these consequences:

- ♥ Unbearable pain
- ♥ Absent-mindedness
- ♥ Insomnia
- ♥ Wide mood swings
- ♥ Crying jags
- ♥ Appetite ups and downs
- ♥ Fatigue
- ♥ Suicidal thoughts
- ♥ Inability to think straight
- ♥ Poor judgment
- ♥ Physical illness, real or imagined
- ♥ Irrational fear

Shock

One second I was thinking, "Everything is normal," because my mind couldn't digest all the pain at one time. Then I would swing totally over to the other side, and the reality of the situation would become present again, and the pain and shock would start all over again. It would come in waves. If the human mind were to have to digest all of that pain at one time, it probably would kill us—the pain is that debilitating.

The grief process is the most intense, exquisite pain of all … and when it's your child for whom you're grieving, it seems to be manifested one-hundred fold.

Our minds take refuge in shock and being numb to it all in the beginning, and then slowly but surely it begins to unfold. Then, in no particular order, I worked through these feelings:

Disbelief and Denial

How could that have happened to my child? I asked myself. They have to be talking about someone else. Can't believe it. Won't believe it! Parents just want the pain and thoughts to stop. You want your reality back the way it was before the "accident." At the time, that was the only way I could tell anyone what happened when describing the incident that took my son's young life.

Guilt

I saw my Chris in every child who bore any resemblance to him at all. The guilt associated with the death of a child is overwhelming at times. The "If only…" and the "What if…?" are constant companions in your thoughts.

What I say to a newly bereaved parent is, "If you could have done anything at all to have prevented the death of your child, you would have done it."

Guilt is an "empty emotion," yet one of the most powerful and draining, and one of the feelings that seems to stay around the longest. The frustration. The pain. You want to die. Can't die. There are others who need you. What about my other children? I'd better not let them out of the house. *What if*—something happens to them?

Anger

The anger and upset feeling you have when other people tell you, "It will be fine." "He's in a better place." "He's with God, and that's where he belongs!" What? He belongs here—with me, his mother, and with his dad and sisters and brothers.

Another saying that upset me was—"God gives you only what you can handle."

What does that have to do with Christian, my tormented mind would cry?

Angry at God. At whomever, except your child. How could she have let him out in the middle of the street? How could she not have seen the gardener's truck coming at him?

It was more than ten years before I could let my anger toward this woman be released. It was many years before I allowed myself to realize that I was angry at Chris. How could I be angry at my Chris when he wasn't here anymore? Hadn't I taught him to look both ways? And I had to allow myself to feel that anger before it would finally begin to go away.

Suicide

Another strong and frightening thought. At times, I wished I could just rip my head off to stop the insane thinking. If I stopped living, then I could be with Chris. If I stopped living, then the pain would also stop. But then what about my other children?

Going Crazy

I was afraid to tell anyone how I felt, fearing that they'd come and take me to a mental hospital. Horrible mood swings. One moment I was thinking, "Whew, I'm going to make it to the next moment," and then the wave of total despair hit again. It came at me like the ocean's waves, in and out.

Fear

As the days and the weeks and then the months begin to unfold, time moves a little more rapidly, because in the first months it seems as if time has literally stood still. I was so stuck with my pain and fear that I thought the world had stopped turning.

Then came the fear of what could happen to my other children. I was sometimes afraid that I would die and sometimes afraid that I'd live. How rational was that? I knew I'd never be the same, but I feared that life would never again be worth living. I feared for my own survival and my sanity.

Random Thoughts

People say and do some of the most insensitive things. They mean well, but in my journey through grief, I discovered that people simply don't know what to say to bereaved parents. Not even members of my immediate family knew.

My brothers and sisters and extended family cried with us, of course, but there was no comfort to be found, and there wouldn't be for a very long time. Why are the birds singing? Why are people laughing? Don't they know my Christian is gone forever?

But, I am here to tell you that

You Will Survive and You Will Smile Again

♥

Chapter 8

♥

Living Through the Grief

Grief following the death of a child is perfectly normal, but it is unique to each person. Do not try to ignore or avoid grief thinking that that will make everything all right. Grieving is necessary. "That which you resist will persist!"

The thoughts that follow relate to a number of subjects you're likely to encounter as you work through your grief and pain. I include ideas and suggestions to help you through this intensely difficult process.

Passage of Time is Important

It has been said that "Time heals all wounds." That is not necessarily true, since we may never heal completely. But the passage of time does dull the pain and help us to understand the feelings that accompany our loss. It is important to *be patient*. Intense grieving has its ups and downs and can be expected to last six months to two years or longer.

Crying

Crying is a healthy expression of pent-up feelings. It is not only normal and acceptable but can be good for you. Cry whenever you feel the need, and don't feel ashamed or embarrassed.

Dealing with Exhaustion

Grief drains you physically and emotionally. You may need to pamper yourself in order to replenish yourself. You'll probably need more rest than you did before.

Do whatever makes you feel better. Nap when you feel like it, take a hot bath, or get a massage—anything that promotes relaxation. Get involved in a project—perhaps one to help others. Exercise, even if it's only a walk in the park or around the block. Take a trip.

After a while, you might want to go to a movie or out to dinner with friends or family members, something to get you in different surroundings. When you can concentrate, read a book, or lie in the sunshine, whatever you love to do for relaxation and diversion. *Follow what feels healing to you and connects you to the people and things you love.*

Insomnia and Loss of Appetite

Physical reactions to a death may include sleeplessness and loss of appetite. A balanced diet, rest, and moderate exercise are especially important for you at this time.

I lost my appetite entirely, and lost almost thirty-five pounds in the first year of grieving. Some bereaved parents might overeat.

Upon falling asleep, I would awaken and end up walking the floors all night, because I was unable to stay asleep, and when I did wake up, my first thought was, "Is this a dream?" Then the reality of what happened to Chris would hit me all over again.

The mind has a tendency to block out the pain and misery for short periods of time; then, when the reality hits again, and it seems to come in waves, we are hurled back in time to when the incident first occurred, and the pain is so intense that it feels as if we will never recover.

Friends and Relatives

When we were finally able to go out with friends, my husband and I began to notice that the moment the subject of "Our Chris" would come up, there would be a silence that I felt I could cut with a knife.

No one, it seemed, wanted to talk about "what happened," when that was all my Jess and I wanted to talk about. We wanted to know that our little man hadn't been forgotten, when what was really going on with our friends was that they simply didn't know what to say to us as bereaved parents, for fear of bringing us further pain and suffering. Little does anyone realize that if your grief is not looked at and dealt with, it can remain your constant companion for years.

Friends and relatives want to help ease your pain, but they don't always know how. Give them some slack if they seem to be uncomfortable around you. Help them to be supportive of you. Talk about your loved one so they know it's okay with you.

Brothers, sisters, and grandparents also grieve deeply and need to feel love and affection as well.

Sharing and Caring

You need to find someone with whom you can share your grief so it doesn't stay bottled up. It might be a family member or it might not. Their lives go on, often in a different direction than yours. Professional counseling may help. Finding a person or a group with a similar experience can be the best therapy of all. You'll know you're not alone and that your expressions of grief are understood and accepted. And you'll be helping others through their grief at the same time you're being helped.

Give sorrow words: the grief that does not speak
Whispers the o'er-fraught heart, and bids it break.

—William Shakespeare, *Macbeth*

Holidays and Anniversaries

Holidays and the anniversaries of a loved one's birth and death can be very stressful. Allow yourself and others time and space for each person's emotional needs on these difficult days.

Faith and Beliefs

Faith and beliefs might be called into question at this time. It's entirely normal, so don't be upset if you find yourself questioning your long-held beliefs. Faith can help many to deal with this unimaginable event.

Decisions

Do not rush into making major decisions such as moving or changing jobs. You won't be thinking clearly for some time, probably at least a year. Changes that now seem right to help you ease your pain and loneliness may be regretted later when your clarity of thought returns, as it will.

Avoid hasty decisions about disposing of a loved one's belongings. You, and you alone, should decide when the time is right and what to keep. Often, well-meaning friends or relatives try to take over this decision. As good as that might seem at the time, it's rarely a good idea. You can do it little by little when you're ready.

Relationships / Vulnerability

You are particularly vulnerable at this time. Be extremely careful of becoming involved in intense relationships. It's easy to feel deeply grateful for a helping hand. Go slowly to make sure it's truly helping you.

There are unscrupulous people who will fake empathy to take advantage of you. Do, however, go out and have warm relationships. You deserve to be as happy as you can be.

Occupation

If you have a job, keep it. Return to work as soon as you feel able. If you don't have a job, you might consider looking for one or for volunteer work. Keeping busy can provide structure in your life when little else seems meaningful.

Hopelessness

You might think that you have nothing to live for. You might think about a quick release from the intense pain. Many bereaved parents think these thoughts. Hang in there—a sense of purpose and meaning does return eventually. The pain does lessen.

Hope

Please know that bereaved parents do recover. My own experience and that of the thousands I have counseled is proof of that. Learning this is one great value of finding a person or group with a similar experience to share with.

Avoid Drugs and Alcohol

Drugs and alcohol are not helpful. In fact they retard the healing process. Many substances are addictive and can lead to chemical dependency. Medication should be taken with caution, and only under the supervision of your physician.

Guilt

Guilt is a normal part of the grief process. Guilt is almost always imaginary. We engage in thinking "If only" or "What if…?" If only I had done this, then this terrible thing wouldn't have happened. In an overwhelming majority of cases, this is simply not true. But, in every case, if there was anything that we could have done to prevent the death of our child, we would have done it. You *must* come to terms with your guilt, and the final resolution must be to forgive yourself. Every one of us deserves forgiveness.

Anger

Anger is another normal part of the grief process, and it must be released if the healing process is to proceed. Anger always arises. Anger is a stage of grief. It needs expression and sharing in a healthy manner. But anger unduly prolonged can scar the heart and delay recovery. In the end, we need to *let it go.*

Security

It is important to reduce stress as much as possible at this time. Try to find help for financial difficulties. Try to relax and get close to those you trust. You can help yourself become more secure by getting back into your routine at your own pace.

Accepting Care

Throughout this time of need, permit yourself to accept expressions of love and caring from others, however awkward those expressions may be. Accept your own feelings. Expressing them is a healthy outlet, and will probably give you insight into yourself, your feelings, and your needs.

Marriage

One of the greatest sorrows I saw in Heartfelt was the difference between the way the mother experiences the death of her child and the way the father experiences his grief. It's not the same. Mothers and fathers grieve in different ways, and must allow one another the space to grieve on their own, in their own way and in their own time. If this is not done when a child dies, many marriages break apart.

Fathers' Grief

Fathers have a "macho image" that leads them to believe that they can't or mustn't cry. They have to hold the family together. They must be strong, when all the while they too feel as though they're dying inside. *Fathers need to talk just as mothers do.*

It's best to join a support group even if you choose never to speak. It helps to hear that someone else is experiencing the same feelings. Fathers see themselves as the family protector, and when that role is invalidated, so are they. Many fathers who have not previously spoken of their grief open up in the group setting.

I can remember fathers feeling "jealous" of the attention paid to the mother, and it does appear that our society sympathizes more with the mother than the father in time of loss.

Small Pleasures

Value every opportunity to allow yourself to feel pleasure. Again, start with small things like a walk in the park or a trip to the beach, or listening to good music. Allow yourself to have fun and enjoy laughter. This will help you to slowly regain more of your happiness later on.

Goals

For a while we have no goals, since life seems to have lost its meaning. This is when we need to set goals for ourselves, beginning with small ones. This gives us something to look forward to, like a short trip next weekend, or a movie tomorrow night, or going to a baseball game with a friend. It's normal at first if you don't enjoy these things as much as you did before, but they're a start and can help you get through one day at a time. As time goes by, you can make long-range goals, giving direction and structure to what may feel like an upside-down life.

Expect to Backslide

As you work through your grief, you're likely to feel that you're making great progress, but something suddenly brings back the pain and despair you felt at the beginning. So, you dig deep inside and work again toward recovery, and later you're set back again. You can expect these ups and downs in the healing process: it's sort of "two steps forward, one step back." But never give up. In the end, you will prevail.

This verse by an anonymous author says it very well:

A New Life

Just when you are making great
strides forward, you receive a
startling setback.
It may happen on a holiday,
birthday, anniversary.
Or it may be triggered by your
favorite song being played on the radio.
You think you are back to where it
all started —
at the bitter moment of death
But remember, anguish like
ecstasy, is not forever.

You Will Survive and You Will Smile Again

Chapter 9

♥

You'll Know You're Getting Better When...

When you begin experiencing *some* of the feelings below, you'll know that you're on the road to recovery. You'll know you're getting better when...

- ♥ You can hear a baby cry without falling apart.
- ♥ You're no longer feeling as guilty.
- ♥ You're not as intensely angry about your loss.
- ♥ You've accepted your loss and are dealing with it.
- ♥ You still cry but not as often.
- ♥ You remember more happy times with your child.
- ♥ You find yourself laughing more often.
- ♥ You're setting more long-term goals and making plans.

- You can look at photos and watch old movies of your child without breaking down.
- You can speak of your child with joy.
- You can speak about how it happened without losing it.
- You can celebrate holidays and anniversaries.
- You can listen to music that reminds you of your child.
- You realize you're not going crazy.
- You know that you still have much to live for.
- Your appetite and your enjoyment of food return.
- You don't have to go to the cemetery as often.
- You can sleep through the night without medication.
- You aren't always tired.
- You can enjoy the beauty of nature.
- You can overlook and forgive inappropriate statements made by others.
- You can think of things other than your loss.
- You can concentrate on other things once again.

You Will Survive and You Will Smile Again

Chapter 10

♥

Getting Complete with Your Loved One

As you work your way through your grief you will gradually improve. You'll probably reach a point where you're ready to get complete with your dear child who is no longer with you.

It may begin with going through his or her belongings, lingering over favorite items, and deciding which to keep and which to dispose of.

You might want to review your life with your child in a bittersweet way. This could include looking at old pictures or movies of your family when he or she was still with you, treasuring every memory of the good times and even the bad ones. It will be helpful to include other family members in this review. For at least ten years I couldn't bear to look at home movies or listen to the tape of my Chris reciting some poems. Don't beat yourself up if the same is true for you.

There are probably many things that you'll wish you had said to your child while he or she was still alive. Say them now. Write them down in a letter and read them aloud to your child, perhaps in some special place you shared. You might have a special place where you feel free to release your feelings—the cemetery, the beach, the desert, or the mountains.

Include in your letter things you would like to have done (or not done) with your child. Tell or ask your child everything you would like to tell or ask.

Say goodbye in some symbolic way, such as burning your letter and watching the ashes go upward into the sky, or releasing a balloon and watching it rise heavenward.

Although we never truly say "goodbye," this open expression may help to give ourselves permission to resume as normal a life as possible.

You Will Survive and You Will Smile Again

♥

Chapter 11

♥

The Grieving Process: A Summary

1. The grieving process takes longer than is generally understood—six months to two years or longer.
2. Grief is an individual process—no two people grieve in the same way. There is no right or wrong way to grieve.
3. The stages of grief occur for all of us, but in no particular order. They are:

- ♥ Shock
- ♥ Denial and disbelief
- ♥ Guilt
- ♥ Anger
- ♥ Feelings of going crazy
- ♥ Despair – nothing to live for

- ♥ Overwhelming sadness
- ♥ Emotional numbness

4. You will likely experience:
   - ♥ Unbearable pain
   - ♥ Absentmindedness
   - ♥ Insomnia
   - ♥ Wide mood swings
   - ♥ Crying jags
   - ♥ Appetite ups and downs
   - ♥ Fatigue – exhaustion
   - ♥ Suicidal thoughts
   - ♥ Inability to concentrate or think straight
   - ♥ Poor judgment
   - ♥ Physical illness—real or imagined
   - ♥ Irrational fear

   All of these are normal—you are not going crazy.

5. Well-meaning friends and relatives may say insensitive things. They simply don't know what to say, so forgive them.
6. It's normal and healthy to cry. Give yourself permission to cry.
7. Find at least one person you can share your grief with. A grief support group can be helpful.

8. Holidays, birthdays, and anniversaries can be difficult times. Do your best to make them happy times.
9. Faith and beliefs can be questioned at this time. If your faith helps you, embrace it.
10. Do not rush into important decisions. You won't be thinking clearly at this time.
11. You'll be emotionally vulnerable for a while, so avoid becoming involved in intense relationships too soon.
12. You and only you should decide whether and when to dispose of your child's belongings. Don't be hasty in making these decisions.
13. Keep busy. If you have a job, keep it, and return to work as soon as you feel able.
14. You still have much to look forward to. Don't let temporary despair lead you to unhealthy thoughts about a quick way out.
15. The use of drugs and alcohol does not help the healing process. Instead, it retards progress.
16. Come to terms with your feelings of guilt. Forgive yourself.
17. Let go of your anger as soon as possible. Express your anger in a healthy way, and don't prolong it unduly.
18. Accept expressions of love and caring from others.
19. Express and accept your own feelings.
20. Mothers and fathers grieve differently. Allow your spouse to grieve in his or her own way and at his or her own pace.

21. Allow yourself to enjoy small pleasures. Have fun and laugh as soon as you are able.
22. Set goals for yourself—modest and short-term at first, progressing to larger and longer term.
23. Expect to backslide: recovery is "two steps forward, one step back."
24. Eventually, you will reach a point at which you know you're getting better.
25. At some point you'll want to get complete with your loved one. You'll want to say goodbye to the extent that you're able to.
26. Remember the forgotten grievers—brothers, sisters, grandparents. They too need love and support.
27. Your life might never be the same again, but you will recover to the point where you'll feel that life is good and the future has meaning.

You Will Survive and You Will Smile Again

♥

I Think About You

I think about you every day
I think about you at night, and
Sometimes when you're on my mind
I think about your life.
Though you'll never grow tall and touch the sky
Never look deep into a woman's eyes.
I know you'll see it; 'cause you're
Looking through my eyes.
You'll see it through my eyes.
The love we shared,
You shared with me
The love you gave to all of them
I think about the change you made
The change you made in all our lives.
Though you'll never grow tall and touch the sky
Never look deep into a woman's eyes
I know you'll feel it,
You'll feel it when I cry
You'll feel it when I cry
Though you'll never grow tall and touch the sky
Never look deep into a woman's eyes
I know you'll see it, you'll see it when I cry
You'll see it when I cry,
I think about you —
I think about you —
I think about you.

— Steven Barton

In loving memory of his brother, Christian Jay Miller

♥

Resources

♥

The Compassionate Friends

PO Box 3696, Oak Brook, IL 60522-3696. 877-969-0019 or 630-990-0010. Assists families following the death of a child of any age from any cause. Nearly 600 chapters nationwide, each providing support, groups, and newsletters. **www.compassionatefriends.org**

SHARE Pregnancy and Infant Loss Support, Inc.

St. Joseph Health Center, 300 First Capitol Drive, St. Charles, MO 63301-2893, 800-821-6819 or 636-947-6164. SHARE offers support to those who have suffered the death of a baby through early pregnancy loss, stillbirth, or newborn death. **www.nationalshareoffice.com**

Sudden Infant Death Syndrome Alliance

1314 Bedford Avenue, Suite 210, Baltimore, MD 21208. 800-221-7437. The mission is to ensure the elimination of SIDS through research and education while offering support to those affected by an infant death. **www.sidsalliance.org**

National Sudden Infant Death Syndrome Resource Center

8280 Greensboro Drive, Suite 300, McLean, VA 22102
866-866-7437

Information services on SIDS and related topics, as well as help with reference and referral services.
www.sidscenter.org.

Vehicular Homicide

Mothers Against Drunk Driving

511 East John Carpenter Freeway, Suite 700, Irving, TX 75062, 800-438-6233.

MADD will put you in contact with an advocate who'll provide comfort, help, and guidance. Many affiliates offer support groups where victims can meet other families who share the experience of an impaired-driving accident.
www.madd.org.

Suicide

American Association of Suicidology

4201 Connecticut Ave. NW, Suite 408, Washington, DC 20008, 202-237-2280. The AAS provides referrals to support groups for the survivors of suicide victims.
www.suicidology.org.

Grief in General

American Association of Retired Persons (AARP)

601 E St. NW, Washington, DC 20049, 800-424-3410. AARP Grief and Loss Programs offer a range of resources and information on bereavement issues for adults and their families. Services include one-to-one peer outreach, a grief course, bereavement support groups, booklets and brochures, and online support.
www.aarp.org.

American Self-Help Clearinghouse

Publishes the Self-Help Sourcebook Online, a database providing information on more than 900 national and international self-help support groups, ideas for starting groups, and opportunities to link with others to develop new groups.
www.selfhelpgroups.org.

Growth House, Inc.

Offers access to the Internet's most complete collection of reviewed resources for end-of-life care.
www.growthhouse.org and **info@growthhouse.org.**

HOSPICELINK (Hospice Education Institute)

3 Unity Square, Machiasport, MN 04655-0098. 800-331-1620 or 207-255-8800. Maintains a computerized database and up-to-date register of all hospice and palliative care programs in the United States. Most hospice programs provide bereavement care in their community; your loved one need not

have been a hospice patient for you to participate in these bereavement services.
www.hospiceworld.org.

National Hospice and Palliative Care Organization (NHPCO)

1700 Diagonal Rd., Suite 625, Alexandria, Virginia 22314, Tel: 703-837-1500, Fax: 703-837-1233, nhpco_info@nhpco.org.

This is the largest nonprofit membership organization representing hospice and palliative care programs in the United States. It is committed to improving end-of-life care and broadening access to hospice care in order to enhance quality of life for the dying and their loved ones. The website helps locate your local hospice for bereavement care.
www.nhpco.org.